by Michael McClure

MICHAEL McCLURE

RARE ANGEL
(Writ With Raven's Blood)

Black Sparrow Press·Los Angeles·1974

LIBRARY OF CONGRESS CATALOGING IN PUBLICATION DATA

McClure, Michael.
    Rare angel (writ with ravens blood)

    A poem.
    I. Title.
PS3563.A262R3   811'.5'4   73-19944
ISBN 0-87685-196-0
ISBN 0-87685-195-2 (pbk.)

Cover from a Verifax print by William Jahrmarkt.

for William Jahrmarkt

FOREWORD

Rare Angel tracks vertically on the page and is Oriental in that way. The selves that comprise our whole being may play over this poem, as if it were a tape, and make prints and new codings. The selves can reach out and speak as the pages move past. The book gives birth to itself from the substrate by writing out muscular and body sensations which are the source of thought.

Rare Angel is about the interwoven topologies of reality. It reaches for luck—swinging out in every direction. It is about the explosion going on.

Walking the city streets the old buildings sink into non-existence and the new buildings rise up. The flow of change is palpable and exciting. It is thrilling to be in this waste and destruction and re-creation. That is one the sensualities of American culture. Our primate emotions sing to us in the midst of it. No one grants credit for the brilliance we burst in.

Whitehead says, "But when mentality is working at a high level, it brings novelty into the appetitions of mental experience. In this function, there is a sheer element of anarchy. But mentality now becomes self-regulative. It canalizes its own operations by its own judgements. It introduces a higher appetition which discriminates among its own anarchic productions. Reason appears."

—And *Rare Angel* appears like an organism with dark eyes, and bristly spotted fur and shining teeth. It is comprised, as our cells are, of Pleistocene hunts and toy umbrellas.

—MICHAEL MCCLURE

"If the origin of life was a step-by-step capsulation of molecules in the sea . . . the earliest forms must have been so large and had so little structure that they left little in the fossil record."

H. T. ODUM, *Environment, Power, and Society*

RARE ANGEL

AND SO WE STRETCH OUT

(it is a muscular sensation
from the neck and shoulders
through the arm . . .

AND SO WE STRETCH OUT
and raise ourselves above our own
black factories.
And we are not in search of poetry but luck
that is ten-trillion Milky Ways
that make a molecule within our chest
or a billion feathered songs sung
from horseback on a bison hunt
WHERE BEAMS OF LIGHT
flash here and there
and make new colors out of dust
that we emit in Fields of Thought.

THEN I KNOW THAT I AM NATURE
where e'er I walk
or drink or think.
I AM THIS SWART PEARL
of Space
TURNED
INSIDE
OUT!

ALL STRANGE STRIPED
CREATURES SLITHERING
through the roots
grin and dance
TO
NEW MUSIC.
I am THEY or THEM!

13

AND
NOW
I am the man within this movie hall
where samurai are slashing with their swords
and flashlights play upon the concrete walls
and toilets smell like modern kitchens.

AND
I can NEVER let myself
go wild, for I remember
I AM ALL.
BUT NOW I AM CLEARER THAN THE CLOUD I EVER WAS.
NOW I AM HERE AND SMILINGLY BELIEVE
EACH THING.

SURELY YOU KNOW THIS IS ME. I CAN BE
told by my naked cock standing up
as I leap through space and fall
on everything I am. LIKE YOU,
WE
are all
and *everything*.

WOLF VIOLETS HOWL!

DREAMS OF OCTOBERS STRANDED ON
BLACK SHALE BEACHES.

Blackberries lying in snow.
Giant snapping turtles in hot, muddy water.
Fingers crossing the moon.
Scent of jasmine.
Tongue on flesh of cling peaches.

GRANDMOTHERS AND GRANDFATHERS FUCKING.
It is all as lovely

AS

A

PIECE
of fluff
THAT FLOATS.

.

.

.

.

.

.

.

.

.

.

.

.

.
.
.

THIS IS THE STUFF! WE ALWAYS KNOW IT IS.

THIS IS THE EXPLOSION
happening all
around us . . .

WE CREATURES
AT OUR CAVE LIPS . . .
(selves are caverns)
hang
down, draped
from ourselves
like waves,
or
stand up
like scarlet mushrooms
in the glowworm's light,

or swim
in cold
rivers underground
through the limestone
made of dots
formed in star clusters . . .

HELLO. HERE IS MY HAND I REACH TO YOU.
(It is something like a paw.)

THIS HUGE PIECE FLASHING BY
IS A CITY MIMING LIFE!

The sword slashes
through nineteen
bodies
—it is one
dream
of what

17

we want.

YOU

KNOW

ME

BECAUSE

I'M
WATCHING

YOU.

You have toes and breasts.

YOU COULD SAY I
wish to be
gentle, sweet, and lovable,
and that would be true, but it
would
stifle
all that matters

if it
became
a code
to live by

WHILE
all this

happens!

Faces peeping from rocks.
Clusters of nothing forming particles.
Rainbows over daisies.
Men watching eagles.
Coils of being turning
to new scents.

MESSAGES IN SEARCH OF SUBSTRATE.

Black zebras swallowing rubies.

Night hawks by barns.

AND THEN PICTURE THE FIELDS THAT STREAM
FROM THAT,
and the clouds they make—or squirms of energy
and relationship. I know
that it *cannot* be
distorted.
It all (as it explodes
or creates

itself—
or
anything)
is surely the messiah. I
fly by
without moving
in it.

Steady,

steady.

STEADY AS SHE GOES!

AND THEN I AM SITTING IN THIS WHITE TRUCK
AT THE CURB OF NOWHERE
where the rug is blood
AND
I
watch for you
because you'll know me.
And that is anthropoid or hominid
to always watch for ourselves
in the other's eye. To always
seek a mirror in hope that it will
FLATTER.
We
SCATTER
in the endless search

for trophies of the instant
because
they taste so sweet

but
it is
better
yet

to crack the scroll of time
instead!

— — — — — — — — —

AND REACH INTO IT AS WE STRETCH!

WE

ARE
REAL

DRAGONS
OF OUR LUCK.

We swirl out what we are and watch for its return.

AND THE PHARISEES BRAND US WITH
TORTURED WORDS
in hope that they'll cause us anguish
for the grief we've hurled
(unknowingly
or
not)
at them. They drift
around like twisted demons.
MESSAGES OF SEXUAL JOY
we never asked for
(and
are
lies)
slither up and down the walls
in formless colors outlined
only
by the shapes of our desires.

WHILE THE WAR DRAGS ON
and little tufts of smoke
in passing eyes
remind us of the sizeless nearby battlefield.

.

Mutate into albinos.
Everything is cut
away
that was useless.
What's left
is
turned
to
new
nerves.

WE KNOW *THAT* IS HAPPENING TO US

((OR THE OPPOSITE))!

EVERY EXPOSURE

to

new condition

is our interwinding
with the welcoming messiah.
EACH
MOUNTAIN
is
a
breast
we fall upon.

IT IS NOT ENOUGH TO SAY THAT EVERYTHING IS US.
YOU ARE AS CLOSE AS MY TOUCH.
FUR.
MUSK.
MAROON PLUSH IN DARKNESS.
Scent of popcorn.
Rivulet of blood.
White buildings in the shroud of fog.
Amphipods in the icy tide.
Fronts of buildings with their back ends torn away.
Black man who sells me cola in his cave.
Angered
child.
Everything
winds in and out
in imitation
of our gut—
or vice versa!
It's more than we can know, except
by rubbing on it.
THERE
ARE
CONCEPTS
just beyond
our grasp
and we're always
at their edge,
when we care to be.
(And I cannot help but care
to be,
for that's my pleasure
and my claim
to what I see.)

TOUCH OF COLD WIND IN BRIGHT SUNLIGHT.

Smell of oil.

Dead fish on cracked ice

and

light *almost* trapped within the sun.

MEMORIES FROM ICELAND MIXED WITH IMAGININGS OF INDONESIA.

GUN
KNIFE
LIFE
STUN
BUN
STRIFE
WIFE
FUN
STAR
TOMB
BOOK
FAR
WOMB
LOOK,
everything is flowing,
everything can see . . . All waves
have eyes!
Literature and life can melt together!

Crows float in air over douglas fir trees.

Thrones of carved jade in mountain caverns.
Smell of ponds in springtime.
(Darting of the pollywog.)
Daddy longlegs caressing in the moonlight.
Pressure of moonbeams on surf.
Red macaws sacrificed in clouds of copal incense.

Fractured surfaces of flint made into an edge.
Towers spouting oil.

Speeding tortoises of metal.
Eyes and nose holes moving on flat walls.

Miracles present themselves
for our benefit and we make
of them what we will.
WE
NEED
TO KNOW
that all these separations
make one thing,

or to learn about the illusion that we call *one*.
Or to see, like Kilroy, over the edge of something.

RAVEN'S FEATHER. EAGLE'S CLAW. EVERY
SONG EVER CHANTED
by the whale hunter
is a collector's item
and wafts like mountain fog
from node to node before becoming clouds.
EVERY
BACKWARD
LOOK
puts us in touch with sentiment,
and hurts less than peering forward,
for tomorrow is the shadow of today.
Even the blue jay
gloats over his stash
of brass buttons. See the octopus play
with the exoskeleton
of his prey.

The statement's convolution
confounds what is already done.

Bulldozed hillsides.

Scarlet flower bugles on the mountain top
overlook the graveyard.

Such elegant music when we make it
(for poets call it music)
surprises
US
in the act
of what we do.
The hand plays hide and seek
with the eye, and we grow
great brains
in honor of the game.
Then we dance and the music

29

follows at our footsteps
and we stop to listen
as it passes by.
WE
HEAR
THE MUSIC
OF
our selves!

Call it animal nature—or name it Civilization.

SPARROW HAWK SKULLCAP. LIGHTNING BOLT
THAT PASSES
THROUGH THE HAND.
WAVES OF CREATURES FLOATING
AT THE EDGE OF FIRE
dive into the air and bound
through space with grace
we nearly comprehend.

Bodies: brown and black and white all blended.
Hoofed and leaping.

TURQUOISE.

CHROME!

Berries and Packards all exploding, lined
with fur of force fields.

DESTRUCTION UNROLLED UPON THE PLEISTOCENE
where we stride in luscious comfort,
and love our children,
hug our pets,
experience
the
alchemy of being.

THE FEW OF US LIKE WAR CHIEFS
AND LOVE-GOD PRINCES
STAND ON THE PRECIPICE WITH FOLDED ARMS.
THIS
LIFE
has
been

nothing

for
me
but

31

pleasure.

The worst adversity
is only a length
I measure.
I direct creation of my bed of eider blackness
and drink the juice of apples
as I sup on flesh of crabs.
I
hold great minds
that lived before me
in my hands.
I KNOW THE MEANING OF THE POWER
THAT IS CHANNELED FOR ME. AND I
calmly watch the poisons
splashed across the land.

I HAVE CUT THROUGH THE HUMANE SURFACE
and I know all men and women
(and they
know me
for I
am them).
WE POUR FORTH OUR WANTS
in the center of this tornado.
Nothing can tear down
what we are
—we only color it with intellective lies.

I
WAS
RIGHT:
WE
ARE
LOVES AND HUNGERS!!!
—Delicate at moments, murderous and murmurous at other. Our
CRIES

are songs and howls
that we make into the sizzling air.

FOR KNOWLEDGE OF WHAT IS TRULY HAPPENING
(beyond our sense of fingertouch or ear)
we must read the walls
while they stand there
amidst the great unrolling,
and study the positioning
of garnets
on the boulder.

THE RETOPOLOGIZING IS RIGHT NOW! WE ARE WAVES
and Princes
in
the

surge!

LIKE ALL MEN AT ALL TIMES, WE ARE ELF
AND FAIRY FOLK!

HEAVY FOOTED AND LUMPISH OR LIGHT AND
DANCING ON THE FLOCCULENCE OF CLOUDS.
WITH DIM WITS OR EYES BRIGHT AND PIERCING,
the hungers are always all the same.
There is little change
except in the counting of the power
that flows to the lip of our ledge. The same
sacrifices evoke the new gods once again.
Zigzag knife or tracer bullet. Kisses made

between the sheets of a perfumed bed.
Little loving creatures there upon our laps
with big brown eyes.

NEW DRUGS
always in demand
to bring the loving god to hug us
as we dive to him and breathe in the embrace.
BUT
we are the Gods!
And not because we say so
in faustian paranoia. Or because

there is a wish to be.
The gift grew, and Luck
can push it further.

THE URGE TO DO IT FEEDS THE LUST TO GROW
BY MEANS OF SWIRLING
into spaces.
Silver towers in cold sea mist.
Severed arms.
Pink elephants and cherubim holding purple plastic flowers.

THOUGHT
is
a
muscular
sensation
pouring outward like
pseudopods with feathered hoofs.
Each hoof taps at the tacks
that press the scroll of the instant
flat upon the field of nothingness.

OH, HOW BEAUTIFUL!

BEAUTIFUL!

The wolf howl on the frosty night.

The rat upon the branch who eats
the cherry blossoms.

Grinning otter sleeping on the waves.

WE
cannot
be
sure
which constellations
open wide the fields like velvet drapes.
I only
watch. Driving
in it. Parking by
the gray curb
that is a universe
for the sensoriums

of
nematodes.
((Or parking by
the gray curb
that is a universe.))
Or
putting a black boot
in the rippling water
of a childhood day.
Or
hearing rain on an umbrella
in soundless space.

THEN I KNOW I AM NATURE, AS TOPOLOGY
UNROLLS ABOUT ME.
Forests turning
into books and rugs.
Things
are carbonized.
Cinders remain where life was/
but power remains
in the frame
of new shapes.
Till I,
TOLTEC-I
AM CHANGED

and barely recognize
my
chubby past
and well-loved toys.
For now I fool with alchemy
to blast my being
past the explosion's burping edge.
EVERYTHING IS NOW A *REAL* TOY.
HAWK CRY AND TRUCK ROAR
are an open door
to just one
purpose:

TO
FOLLOW
DOWN
WHAT
MY
BODY
KNOWS
and pour out like shoulders
from a neck,

OR
LIE LIKE
A PAIR OF DICE

ON WHITE VELVET,

OR DREAM LIKE BLOSSOMS ON AN APPLE BOUGH,

OR KISS GOOD MORNING TO THE MORNING,

or flow like dew around the nests of sleeping mice!

RACING THROUGH THE TUNNELS UNDER SNOW.

Hailstones the size of apricots.

Children singing in the sundown.

LOVELINESS
OF GOLD FLAKES
SCATTERED INTO ERMINE.

.

OR
AM I A DEMON
with my head thrown
back and mouthing
words from this cave
of faces? Or am I
AN ANGEL
(all sweet and bright)
(warm, solid, real)
with arms crossed
and hands on biceps?

The poem that I'm writing is like a museum of living nudi-branchs (a long line of clown messiahs) describing TOLTEC-ME and baby-me—and the way the surface of the Earth is an energy explosion that removes the Pleistocene and leaves only cinders in the shapes of bookends, rugs, and tractors. And even that (sadly) is a part of my "spiritual" development. So the poem has to rise by making a swooping swing so that the whole is finally (per-haps) a sublime perception locked into itself and reaching out. It is numberless trials that make a conscious and unconscious feedback loop.

A
PALACE FOR LARGE BLACK ANTS
at the base of the walnut tree.

Flick of swords slashing brows.

Flashlight beams playing over concrete.

My imagination
(only)
reaches warmth
across

41

the space.
Who knows what she sees.
The huge hairy animals haul themselves
along the plain and stop and eat
the bushes. By the water hole
men leap up out of silence
swinging clubs and screaming.
The hairy creatures stand in wonder
and terror and faintest
flicker of admiration for the painted faces . . .

SO NOW IT'S SERIOUS,

YOU SAY.

You say it is serious.

You say it pours into itself
like honey poured from cup to cup.

THINGS ARE WHAT THEY ARE:
WAVES OF STARS OR DOTS.

I
KNOW
ALL
THAT!

The net of constellations
is as serious
(or laughable)
as I am.

THE

SILHOUETTE

OF

A

PELICAN

DIVING

BEAK

FIRST

into

WAVES.

Red and gray and blue
reflections flickered back and forth.

Dead friends speaking to me.

Sailing ship mirrored in its own wake.

SAND DOLLARS.

GIANT CACTI.

Huge rivers bursting through the mountains.

WAVES THAT TAKE THE SHAPE OF WATER
cradling the surge of salmon schools . . .

Ripples that take the form of typewriters
or of men . . .

SIGNS THAT SAY:

HOTEL

HOTEL

HOTEL

or almost sentimentally:

Coca-Cola.

Over-replicated children sneer and make love-signs
at one another.
The old high way of thinking in clarity
is drowned by lack of judgment
and now we formulate in clouds
of color, heaps of scents,
and all the textures
planned
by
creative genius.

AHHHHHHHH-H-H-H-H-H-H-H-H-H-H—
we know we're love gods
in pain.

EMPTY HAND REACHING THROUGH SPACE.

THE UPSURGE OF SELF-AFFIRMATION.
Smiles returned by beautiful faces.
Sunbeam gleaming in a dusty room.
Skulls lined side by side upon a table:
man, dolphin, raccoon.

Flying lemurs eating coconut flowers in moonlight.

JET FIGHTERS IN MID-AIR FIRING ROCKETS
AT EACH OTHER.

- -

Flaming horses in the surf.

ANOTHER SPOT—SOMEWHERE
ELSE IN ANOTHER
SWIRL OF SPACE
or
untouchable
dimension
and I am writ upon it in modes of senses
that I do not comprehend.
It's here beneath my foot
or lost behind
another Milky Way.
The fire burns caverns in a cardboard box.
Black edges curl inward in red flames . . .

The sound of surf makes grottos
in my mind. Sand beneath
my elbow. Boulders of silicon
and serpentine and smooth crushed shell.
The helicopter is a bar of ruthless sound
across it all. The fall

TAKES
THE PRISONER
looping thirty thousand feet
with hands bound behind his back
while crowds of feasting gods
are singing his goodbye.
The jay turns over a brass button.

THE MONSTER OPENS HIS BLUNT FACE—EYES WIDE!
Snags of fur blow around his snout
in the savannah wind. Dragonflies
dart away from the water hole. The coppery
horsehair snakes move blindly—and indifferent—
frightening mosquito larvae with the clouds
of sediment. Waterstriders move back
among the cattails. The beast screams wheezingly
with fear and alarm. He raises one clawed
arm—half-turns—shit pours
from him into the pond.
One man rips him open

47

with the flint.
Blood pours like a little waterfall
from a fur mountain.

THEY YELL WITH GLEE
distorting stripes
of ochre and green
upon their faces.

The baby raven listens from his nest
on a nearby cliff.
Vultures think about it overhead.

Two things grow together in the darkness.

AND YET IT IS GREAT LOVE
—REAL PHYSICAL ATTRACTION—THAT MAKES
us what we are.
Each cell is an inheritor
of earlier loves.
NOT
ONE
LOVE
but many formed each cell
of every
being!
Each cashmere gesture reflects it.

Every time I reach or withdraw in kindness.

EVERY PUSSYWILLOW IN THE MARSH
OR MAD VIOLET IN THE MEADOW.

EVERY GIRAFFE AND AUK AND JAGUAR . . .

Every bat and great blue whale
and planetoid
or red giant.

EVERY SET OF GESTURES MARKED FROM ONE POINT
AND STOPPED AT ANOTHER
becomes a cloud
that is a field
in all directions that we know
and many others. And we
write upon it in calligraphy
of what we are. But only
guess how
to reread it.
Then that makes a field within
and all around the other.

THE
SWORD
IS MADE FOR BEAUTY;

DUTY
KILLS.

BUT death is only at one point upon a field.

THE CLOUD IS A MOHAIR SHAPE
of interwoven
constellations
that
comprise
each other.

LOVE AND HUNGER COMPRISE HATRED.
HATRED AND LOVE
join to be hunger. Hatred and hunger are love.
It is a verbal exercise to show
that we
are made
in subtler ways
than our Platonic statements.
Everything
all melted down
and glossy-glassy
becomes an ethic like a green
plastic Parthenon
and

it

WILL

NEVER BEAT

OLD AGE OR DEATH!

No vacuum cleaner or opinion brings escape
or Liberation.

NO GURU
OR
MOSES
BRINGS
you
any
news
but your own winged smile!

— — — — — — — — —

WE ARE AS FREE

                    as
               everything
                 around
                  us!
        Candles burning in the twilight.

        Trucks growling in the dawn.

        Floors rippling in an earthquake.

        Embroidery upon the lips of clouds.

        Thunderstorm above a cornfield.

        Scent of pink silk and encyclopedias.

THE LEOPARD SEAL DIVES UPWARD IN THE WATER
—CRASHES THROUGH THE ICE
AND GRABS THE PENGUIN.

Hot penguin blood on cheeks and whiskers.

Veils of plankton.

Mysterious laughing faces buried in fire, earth, water, air.

"Know thy self."
But the brain is not
truth's organ
and we find
there is no tathagata
but the all
we are.
The cloud is silky sexuality
or solid rock
or
empty nothing
filled
with smiles and frowns.

FREEWAYS GLOW
with their machine gun automatic load:
CAR (*swish*)   CAR (*swish*)   CAR (*swish*) . . .

Our feet grow flat and human
and our hands more soft and subtle.

Then we can bring
out
the hungry tree shrew
with
his
swinging saber
in the darkened room

and move the physiology
of ancient bodies

in patterned colored light.

That is science in the guise of art
or entertainment.

That is all I am.

My trembling
makes me real.

How fine a thing is longing—or a hunger!

AND SYMPATHY IS HATRED FOR THE FAILING SELF.
Sympathy draws one body inside
another (as does hunger)
and makes love—
and many into one.
Genius
grinds all things
into infinite pieces
and scatters
them
in all times and places

with
organic sense
of what it is all about

—and then forgets and has a dream
about
A SILVER EGG.

CIRCLES OF LIGHT MOVE ON THE CONCRETE WALL
in blackness.

The curb in bright sunlight.
Sound of rain on an umbrella.
Abalone shell reflecting dawn.
Shimmering sunlight in a perfect room.
Blissful fantasies adrift.
Honeybee screaming in the dusty
gradeschool window.

Soft leather purse with pennies in it.

Scent of candy stores and clack of castanets.

Deer moving in the mottled shade.

Hunters singing.
.
.

.
.
.
.
.
.
.
.
.
.
.
.
A PENGUIN WALKING ON THE ICE.

AND SO WE STRETCH OUT
and the muscular sensation moves
from neck and shoulders
through the arm
AND
THE
Real Poetry
comes in moments like the dawn
or instances of thoughtlessness
made bright by rich and blank
sensoriums.
Then all things lay themselves out
rich and shimmering
in full pigment
dappled by the light.

.

I MEAN THE BED HAS WINGS AND CARRIES ME.
I smile as casually
as an otter
in the golden sleepy sun.
The wolf-dog in the vacant lot devours a cat
and wags his tail.

WE
LOVE
TO
WALK
THROUGH

ROOMS
OF
WHAT
WE ARE
and know the flesh is shaking in the air.

WE ARE EACH A LOVE GOD
dissolved
into reality

and searching for the frozen furnace
of the dissolution.

EVERY
LITTLE
THING
HAS
VISAGES
AND WINGS
or doesn't.

IT MATTERS TO US WHAT WE ARE AT THIS
(AND EVERY)

FLASHING INSTANT!

THE RABBIT CARES!
AS DOES THE OCTOPUS AND QUARTZ CRYSTAL!
A
hairless, purple head
pokes in from everywhere
and we name it *friend*.
We glide at ninety times the speed of light
on helixes
of hurricanes that pour
into the maelstrom.

We stack old wooden chairs
and put cigarette butts in the lips of moose heads.

I know there is a distance there
between
the I
and you.
Rocketships flash back and forth
from our fingers
in the darkened room.
The landscape is made of the bodies of trees
cut into strips.
There are
fighting people.
The men worship flowers
knowing they are blooms
themselves
and they pluck one another to make bouquets.

IN THE RICH WET CREVICES WHERE EVERYTHING
is just one life
the symbiosis starts.
Everything
coils
over
and
crumples—as if in preparation
for explosion.
Hugs together.
Creates a complex anchor-net.

Hurls itself out—as if to catch
the wings of Time
could matter.

CAN
WE
BE THAT DUMB
AND BEAUTIFUL?

ARE WE ALL FABLED BLONDES OF BLACKNESS
WITH DIAMONDS IN OUR HAIR?

"Why do all the wise beings on earth eat my ass, mine
Antonin Artaud's?"

"And what in hell are we doing here?
Why in hell are we living?
And why are we alive?"

TO
READ
THIS
POEM
!
To pursue our luck
in aggregate complexities
of perception.
¿ To open the chest wide so the Indian band
may pour out whooping in pursuit
of bison?

TO CREATE NEW TERRITORIES IN THE
SHAPES OF HANDS.
(To intertwine, to let all being fly.)

To build the battlefields and No Man's Lands
of Love.

To spray the scent of strawberries into interstellar space?
To coat almonds with smooth sugar.
To hold wet water snails.

—SO THAT *SELF* MAY BE SELF'S MESSIAH
EVERYWHERE!

It
comes slanting
all at once like
electric rain. They say
it does!

. . . . . .

To make a kind of pine cone.

A simple thing of facets.

Less than a buttercup.

Barely alive

but

breathing.

All torn up in new directions everywhere.

"Mass was invented to make human sexuality pass through certain paths." (A.A.)

DÜRER, RAPHAEL, AND SHANG DYNASTY
CRAFTSMAN OF BRONZE.
All are concerned with babes, madonnas,
tigers, owls.
They are
hypnotized by
(*in love with*)
gorgeous
shapes
of moiling intricacy
—and show them flat
or in faint relief.

They leave the eye to move around
in the material mind.

Let the neuron eye-light
flow around
the body of
a sun bear.
Let the eye-light
charge
in no known form
through
no
known blackness.
Let the blackness be indigo and melt in silver.
OUT
OF
IT
COMES THE SHADOW
OF MY FACE
OR YOURS.
It gains dimension
—then becomes a cliff with firs
—then a planetoid.
Now it is a psychic submarine and dives
streaming into
everywhere.
Then it becomes a hand to write with white music
in the shadows.

Cars carve the freeway up with sounds.

When we lose ourselves it is death, and Luck enters.
                    REBORN!

Brown hills flow gently towards
            the mudflats.
      Seals face the sunset.

Limpets under boards.

The antlered worms are artisans of hunger.

WE ARE ADDICTED TO OUR PERSONALITIES.
(I AM!)
What pleasure then to let it go, and slide
away from all the pain.
But
then
WE ARE NOTHING
is the cry—
and that is right.

LOKI GETS THE LAST LAUGH.

We are hollow snakes in nowhere.
If the tanner comes
and takes the skin
then what is left
is the frost giant's grin
reflected on a glacier.

BLACKNESS
splits into two ravens,
Thought and *Memory*.
They
fly
forward
and settle on our shoulders.

The well stares up at us with one eye
and a trillion-billion facets
stir when the hazelnut
of personality drops in.

AND
THEN
THE SALMON LEAPS
AND EATS THE MAYFLY!

Sounds of motorcycles grinding on the peaks.
Feel of Autumn in the air.
Russet ripples.

Maid Quiet walking on the leafy forest floor.

THE CAVE WHERE CHILDREN PLAY
BENEATH THE GIANT STUMP.

And
—like art nouveau—
the black wings
make weird silhouettes
that we see between.
They tell me everything has a name
because the universes rub together.

An apple brushing on a feather.

THE LIKELIHOOD OF PERSONALITY IS IMPOSSIBLE.
BUT PROBABLE!
What other thing
would I have be *me*?
An abstract song sung by asteroids?
A rainy glaze upon a tropic forest
is
what
I am.
And I'm glad.

. . . .

THE NET THAT IS AN ANCHOR AND A SURGE
hurls itself out
as
if
the whole thing matters.
As it does, flames roll from the edges
in extreme slow motion.
It becomes more complex
than an aerial lichen
and the whole thing
catches fire.
WE
ARE
THE
FIRE
MEN!

We
are the eaters in the grassy lands
that enter forests for the sake of Deer.
We have tortured and eaten all warm-blooded
dragons
and sung our crazy songs
and found our corn, squash, wapato,
wheat and rice. We kissed goodbye to the antlered
giraffe and rhino. The last pink-haired
fairy armadillo

68

hides beneath a stone
in secret contact
with the final family of golden lion marmosets.

It
is sweet to be a Prince

with my heel upon this scene.

Boccherini, Mozart, Haydn, seven stringed Ch'in lute tinkle
on my skyhigh porch.

RARE ANGEL, (take a letter)
      PINK RIPPLES ARE WAFTING FROM
      THE LIGHTNING BOLT.
      BLUE CLOUDS FLOAT AROUND IT ALL.
         Horizons separate
         with flesh drifting
         in between.
         Blue-purple waterfalls
         drip down
         upon the fields
         that we
         inhabit.

      Drums beat in the middle distance.
      Cock starlings squeak on roof tops.
      Bearded students lounge
         in damp cafes.

   Envies and hungers beat upon the walls with leaden fists.
      Substances become huge like visions
         and then deplete themselves.
               FIGURES
               FLICK
               INTO
               THE
               AIR
         WITH FLASHING SWORDS!
         Oriental profiles float
         upon the walls.

         And the whole conjoined
         improbable unlikelihood
               flips
               up its edge
               to catch
               at Time
               that passes.
         The explosion
         flows outward from
         each direction.
         The flames

are thawed
in giant
frigidaires.

DARKNESS
and
LIGHT
are
moved
from
place to place
in groaning boxes
filled with broken legs.

RARE ANGEL . . .

BLACK ARTS ARE SMEARED ON APRIL AFTERNOONS
LIKE TOOTHY SMILES
grinned at a fearful dog that cowers behind
a lattice porch.

BABY SMILES.
Taste of drambuie.
Red cottages in mist.
Rowboats on a lake.
Giant logs afloat in surf.
The scent of kelp.
The lives
of sea anemones
on pilings.
The blank,
behemoth
metaphilosophies
of jellyfish
and sea cucumbers.

THERE!
Again I reach for you.
You, being warm and real, insist
that
I
know
what
YOU
think
is beautiful.
And I have no contradiction
but I'll always
search for some
other answer.
Whatever
it may be.

EVERYTHING
is what our senses
make it—
SORTING

THROUGH
THE SMOKE!

Being might slip out of its concealment
to become one thing
once again

OR
it may not.

BUT
you're swirling.

(WHIRLING
and settling like a flock of crows
around a party of blind chimpanzees
on a picnic.)
I can hear the sound but I cannot know
the patterns or the flights.
I can symbolize
but I cannot
speak of it.
I
do not
have the centers
—OR
THE SPIRIT-NEURONS—
to make the stream of words.
I get the message
but I do
not have the screens
to show the pictures.

I
HAVE
BEEN
EVERYWHERE
when it happened.

(It is beginning
to be over.)

The control room
is a stage prop.
Through the windows
we
can
see the sets.
They are real:
rubies, diamonds,
tulips, flames,
and fantasies,
and purple scarves,
and spider webs

74

and chocolate bars.

Only the simplest levers
fit our hands. I can
go up or down
and right and left
and fly and pour
and drip and flash
UNSTOPPABLE
AMONG THE CLOUDY STUFFS THAT MAKE
THIS SOLID THING.

We

know it.

ALL THE WORM TRAILS UNDERNEATH THE BARK
OF A GIANT FOREST
write a name in a script
I cannot translate.
And I do not care to.
Its existence
is a spirit's
secret name
AND
all lives lean
on each other.
They are clean and lean
and well known.
Like a chinchilla-bat with tentacles
they toss out strands
and at their tips
are a billion buffalos
or a fern forest
or the whisker of a ring-tailed cat
that is chewing on a mouse skull.
I
HAVE A MEMORY
OF A FRIEND LYING DEAD
IN A POOL OF BLOOD IN AFGHANISTAN.
A
pistol
in his hand.

He melts back in.

The mountain speaks to me
by being
as
a rose vine does.
Dead friends
are
clear
too.

The jay is gone.
He gloats over buttons.

A RAINBOW ROLLER COASTER.

An elephant's foot umbrella stand
is a sadder thing
than my friend's death.

The eyes of ducklings and their breath.

Gorillas sleeping in the forest.

Glaciers calving icebergs into the Arctic Sea.

ALL THINGS ARE MATTER WHEN MASS ARISES.
That which does not transcend
burrows underneath the Sky's edge.
All the black beetles on the California desert
and all the great blue whales
are real people.

The buckeye butterfly is lovely as a condor.
Hawks migrate above our houses.

Circles of light move over concrete.
Our caves stay open
behind changing faces.
Flames flow
like incandescent
syrup
—heaped up in
waves
and
breakers—
all across the landscape.

Some days
the air
is gray fire.

Brown air
makes bizarre
sunsets.

AURAS

hang

in new

places!

Behind doors
and
over engines.

OLD RADIANCES
begin
to disappear.

Where is the fox fire
in
Jack O'Lantern time?

When will Mr. Frost doodle on the window
with his nippy hands?

NOW WITH MY HANDS UPON THE GEARS
WE ZOOM OUT . . .

JEALOUS OF A WOLF!
I am a monster. You are a monster.
YOU
can be loved
and cuddled like a chick.

Peeping in our incubators.
Stirring in the chrysalis is what we're told
we're doing.
IRISH ELKS SWIMMING THROUGH A SEWER
THAT RUNS BENEATH A CRUMBLING CITY.

Jays perch outside the window—staring in
and laughing.
The horsehair snake makes a shadow in the sun.
He is coppery—a thick wire. He has no mouth
except a groove. He grew in the body
of a cricket—living on the juices in the muscle.
Then he burrowed out through the cricket's shell.
Now warm water is his home. He is a cave
with no eye holes—but he is all sense.
Mosquito larvae dash
from the area of disturbance—where
he makes a tiny cloud of turbulence
from particles of soft gray
and velvety sediment.
The huge furry creature who has been drinking
raises up his head. The cattails
rattle slightly
in
the
wind.

THEY
SAID

THERE IS A SILVER LIGHT
behind all things and that bodies
are the masks we change—as one
might blink his eyes
after a drizzle as he stands in a graveyard
surrounded by a field of rainbows.

And the larvae love the sun and oxygen
and
they
know
all things
around them
move.

THE PREDATORS MAKE PATTERNS IN THE AIR.
Wolf and coyote are oscilloscopes.
The last red wolves are in thickets
to the South.

Mozart playing with the universe.
Boccherini thinking timeless thoughts while mission padres
eliminate the Indians
and put their souls
in pearly boxes.
Ants
celebrating rites
of blackness
in the sweetened air.

ARCHWAYS WHERE THE SUN STREAMS IN!

BOLTS OF LIGHTNING FROZEN IN THE AIR!

SHEWANNAH IN THE SHAPE OF BUFFALO POURING
THROUGH YOUR EAR!

April kissing August in a cave.

The edge lifts up like a lip.
Then it all becomes a sail of finest stuff
—gray French velvet
tinged with pink
embroidered
by
the thought
we hurl toward
it.
And it grows
our mother's face
and smiles
at us
AS
we
always
knew

it would.
Then she says
in kind words
(so sensitive)
that she is roaring
at us
if we would hear her.
She says that she is stroking
us
if we
would remember.

GREEN SEA LETTUCE IN THE TIDE POOLS.

"YOU'RE JUST A BABY IN DISGUISE."

.

"AHA! I AM NOT SURPRISED.
A VAST CAVERN CARVED
OUT OF THE ICE!"

.

And then gray turbulence drifts past a bubble in the mud.
The sun shines back to itself from the water's skin
like a silver tiger leaping all ways at once.
Cattails make dark green shadows.
The image of an osprey in the distance dives
through a ripple.
The sound of a nearby splash.
Slushing suction of huge hairy foot
in mud.
He is as large as a truck.
He bends his head to drink from the shining
water.
Mosquito
larvae
plunge
and
dance
like drunken sirens.

THE SALMON GRABS THE MAYFLY!

*You are tired of being
someone else?*

THE WORLD
we stand in
is an aura
THAT
WE
SHAPE
AROUND

84

US.

All our trails
in it
are
our
last
illusion.

AHA! I AM NOT SURPRISED.
A VAST CAVERN CARVED
OUT OF THE ICE!

YOU'RE JUST A BABY IN DISGUISE!

The first is where the last is once again!

THE GAME IS REAL AS GOLDEN DAYS AND POLYMERS.
Billiard balls in heaven bounce off Pythagoras.
YELLOW FLASHES!
(Clicks of light.)
Garter snakes speeding on green velvet.
Neuron
ripples
catch the drift
of fresh surprise.
LUCK
is
made this way
—and emanates the silhouettes
of vanity at worst.
At best we are reborn each instant
every day
into eternity.
((OR
SOME
OTHER
DELUSION.))

IT IS BEST TO BE HERE AS WE DIVE THROUGH SPACE.
Feel ourselves as the muscles
stretch to make us.
THIS IS TRULY ALCHEMY!
THIS   THIS
IS   IS THE
TRULY   SECRET
ALCHEMY!   BOOK!

And   And

there   there

are   are

STARS
IN
GROANING
BOXES.

Bearded smiles.
Drops of gleaming wax on parchment.
Crickets playing host to gods.
Smells of fresh cut wood.
A figure dancing with a sword.
Men with deer horns.
Breasts on eagles.
Smoke in mist.
Rivers rippling.

Honest lovers' grins.

Beauteous girls in minuet.

SPEAK, OH RAVENS BLOOD.

"WE LOVE THE BODY. WE WISH TO HOLD IT.
THE BODY IS A STONE.
The rock is a body.
The boulder cares.
The gravel stares
with gravity sensors
from underneath
the lithic lid.
WE RUSH TO HUG AND CRUSH AND KISS
THE PRECIOUS THING
that grins at us referring back
itself as homunculus
of what we are.
We do not stare closely. Almost anything
of flesh will do
whether it has scaley tail
or violet wings
or barks or mews.
WE NEED THE MORPHOS AND THE NEWS
it brings us.
It does not fill us with cold rhyme
but with huge warm love
that is nearly
the kind of thing
that Luck is."

WE GRAB THE LOVELY THING AND SPEAK TO IT AS IF
WE WERE A BABY!
The secret language is unveiled.
We always knew it
but
forgot to speak.
AS
WE KISS IT
it becomes an egg
again. A fantastic
sleek, smooth thing
in a bag of water
staring out.

88

A perfect form
with no rough edges

smoothed over

in the river bed

of what someone calls

TIME.

(Lying on scarlet silk sheets.)

OR IN A MULTICOLORED GROTTO . . .
With prints of flowers
that pass through minds of Byzantium
and Han.
Pictures and poems pop from the walls.
Veils of fog drift through the street
and hang outside the casement
where Arabs tamper with *plastique*.

THERE IS A BLUEBIRD FLYING IN THE STONE.

A lion dances on the apricots.

The body shows it is a cloud
by being solid.

Coffee grinders make spinnerets of sound.
A saber slashes through a brow
and the tree shrew
does somersaults
chasing tiny rodents.

THERE!

THERE!

THERE YOU ARE AGAIN!
I have been pursuing tendrils.
We are topologies of cells
and distribution patterns
reduced down
from our projections.
We are auras of visages
that
sing
around

the serpent's tongue.
WE ARE THE VISION
THAT WE'RE SCARED
TO HAVE!
AND HERE WE STAND
with
TOES
and
EARS
like Li'l Abner
or the sacred Khan.

Dancing in the wildwood once again.

WE ARE STICK FIGURES CARVED ON CLIFFS OF STARS
(with swirlings round our heads
that draw us into flesh).
The cash
we pay for things
is the cost of every word.
There are herds
of shaggy beings
in the opal.
One furry thing stands
in the oaky delta where the water runs
in streams. Where the sun beats down
upon cattails. He scratches
at the water's surface with his giant claws.
He looks up with deep-set eyes and sees
the fish hawk.
In the meadow
far behind
are carnivores with snouts.
Long-necked beings stand on the horizon.
The osprey hovers with wings upthrust
and tremulous. The fairytale
of lives begins
and ends
at any point.

Fingers stretch across space
while ships
flash back
and
forth.

The flowered men cry out
like Crazy Horse.

THE SEA PALMS NEED THE SURGE.

Gray mariposa lilies/
furred kitten paws.

Huge mussels.

Rhododendrons in the forest.

Touches on the shoulder.

Girls in tuxedos dance with canes.

Collaborators throwing kisses to their brains.

Sharks' teeth.

HAZELNUTS STRETCHING INTO THOUGHTS.

THE FAIRY RADIANCES THAT HANG IN AIR
ARE SHIELDS ABOUT OUR HEADS.
The floating
falling
leaves
are just
the same.
Your name
is writ
in fair
scratches
and the billowings
of golden dust.
The bedstead and the distant mount
(beneath the radar cones)
and the fireplace
in between
are planes
that fools
and sages
see as
stained glass
peep holes
to
an
other scene.

ALL

THE

OUTRÉ

TELLS

ME

that the universes are
a tear-off jacket of tattoos
all sleeveless
and draped across my shoulders

94

with coconuts for buttons
and a tarantula for bouttonniere!
I
have wings,
and antlers,
hairy legs,
horse's ears,
a giant pizzle,
a drunken father,
AND
A
MORTAR LAUNCHER
FOR A BOW.

YOU WILL KNOW ME BY THE STORIES THAT I TELL!

YOU
WILL
EVEN
KNOW
THAT
WE
ARE
LOVELY
COLTS
STUMBLING
IN
our
first
snow
and leaving prints all over white December
and
tiny ferns
in shadows of big rocks
and scented barns
in empty fields
with
doves
nesting
in
the haylofts
—and a slowly running stream
where catfish dream.

AND SO WE STRETCH OUT
to the white truck
that parks beside the curb
by the universe
near the grotto.
IN
THE
SECTOR
WHERE REAL VISIONS PLAY
ALL OVER CLIFFS.

And the walls clutch themselves
and hug into a capsule like a ball
but they unroll
when we stroll
by.
I
whistle casually
as if I do not know.

I KNOW HOW ALL THINGS WORK AND I AM PLEASED.
I MAKE GREAT BOATS
from cardboard tubes of Quaker Oats
and nails and string
and rubber bands.
To build a crystal palace for the princess
is my game.

My pretty kitten is the champion boxer of the fairy tales.

AND FINALLY
REACHING
IN
THE
CAVE
(or out of it)
THERE IS NOTHING
THAT CAN BE TAKEN SERIOUSLY
OR NOT
and there is no size,
big or small,
that can be measured
on a scale.
We can never smell or taste enough of it.
The walls are marshmallow
covered with chrome
and changed to flesh.
The color of a plum
reflecting back
the seriousness of a forest.
IT
IS
A
FLAME
and a fairy radiance!

Everything increases as it crumples
back upon itself. It gathers
strength
that way
to make
a leap that may
or may not happen.
I RIDE MY WHITE CAMEL—OR MY TRUCK—
ACROSS THE FLAMING DESERT
with the moon behind my turban
chanting songs
of childhood
that
happen
in the future.

CARPETS OF LONG-LEGGED KING CRABS
crawl across the ocean's icy floor.

Kinky hairs float in sunny wind.

Autos honk in tunnels.

Chocolate kisses wrapped in shining foil.

((((
ONCE AGAIN I HAVE REASON TO BELIEVE IN
ALL THE CLOUDS
that make these puffs
of clouds.
I know that they are wrapped
around one another
and wove together
to make a shapeless
Uncarved Block.

WHEN ALL THE PIECES
draw back
there is then the nothing
left behind.
))))

Spots of red fruit
squashed on white clapboard.

Fossil fish
that swim through slate.

Date palms by the oasis.
Lonely tigers growling in their sleep.

St. Francis dancing with the Areopagite
while Plato and Lao Tzu
roar with laughter.

Pink mattresses stacked one thousand high.
Conveyor belts of buckets filled with nectar.

Lobsters cooking.

Cord convertibles
that nap in front of art deco buildings.

Glaciers moving towards
the Kansas seabed.

100

EVERYTHING
all
caught up together
like the beings in a submarine
—and watching

while they writhe and kiss

with silk gloved hands

and
turn on the projector for the final movie.

(Call that the Steam Ship Universe.)

BECAUSE IT IS THE ULTIMATE IN BEAUTY
(and the ONLY)
the many Selves
of us touch it
as we slide by
OR
AS
IT
PASSES
OVER US!

ONLY IN OUR ARROGANCE DO WE ASK FOR
SIMPLICITY AND SHININESS!
It does not gleam except when we distort it.
Then it is like an ancient movie shown
too many times.
All the scratches wear away the nose and eyes
and elbows.
Blurred forms
perform vaguely sexy
duties.
The projectionist
says that this
is either art or pornography.
The sensation pleases
but
outside

(in the explosion)

there is wet fog and the crunch
of autumn leaves.
The sounds of car crashes.
Firetrucks whooping.
Facets in the air like crystal candy.

OLD
MEN
singing to the spirit of the tiger.

Wolves in dens on hillsides.

AWAKENING IN PAINLESS YOUTH AGAIN
but knowing
it is painless youth.

FREE OF ALL DESIRES TO BE A *THING*.

Aware that the mind will not liberate.

On hands and knees chewing on the luscious grass tufts,
clouds in shapes of sages drifting overhead.

THE
SELVES
PRINT
THEM
SELVES:

CAVE
MOUTH
WITH
A
HALO

WINGED
HANDS

FINGERS
WITH
STINGERS
OF
BEES

WASPS
SLEEPING
UNDER
TREES

((Picture-bubble:
a huge beast
drinking from a pond
then killed
by men.))

MARBLE
COOLING
IN
A
MULTICOLORED
PUDDLE

A
HERO

CHOKING
DRAGONS
ON
A
CLIFF

BLUE
MACAWS
DRYING
WET
FEATHERS
IN
THE
SUN

THE ISLE OF OKINAWA IN A MISTY SEA—A PUFF OF ROCKY TURBULENCE.

TUESDAY.

FRIDAY.

Drinking wine from tiny cups.
Anemones that tremble in the wind.

White hibiscus growing on the riverbank.

Desert poppies on a gray-green bush.

The buildings disappear and tall ones rise
and make excitement.
I can
feel the change
about me. Thrill
comes charging through
the skin. The
air roars silently
over many years.
We
gather
it
as
we
walk
by
and grin.

This Power distills ennui into an intoxicant.

.

THIS AXE SHINES.

A hand hangs there in space.

The air is a living cloth of sounds.

The fall and rising of the buildings
leaves a charge
in space.
It
is all another bubble
on the ripple's edge.

The escalator floats me
to the wave.

AND SO I RISE
TO
WHERE
THE
EAGLES WHEEL
IN SQUADRONS!

AND
SO
I
pass
by
the
ivory
statuette
of
reality!

The speeding space ships hang forever steadily
immobile.
Men make guttural shouts and swing their swords.
Slashing
through the brow.
Circles of light play upon the concrete walls.

We hold it in our palms
and crush and kiss
it
all at once.

I TELL YOU THIS IS BEAUTY!

YOU TELL ME THIS IS BEAUTY!

We
ache as if we're smashed
by parts of us.

WE WISH TO BELIEVE.

OUR

DISBELIEF
IS
PAIN.

WE'RE STRETCHED
—STRUNG-OUT LIKE BUBBLE GUM!

EVERYTHING WE'RE SUPPOSED TO KNOW
GRABS OUT AT US:
social loves,
Chevrolets
and *Boccherini!*

———————————

We sail right on past—free as sun fish!

BUT
WITH THE STEADY ACHE
THAT KNOWLEDGE CARVES IN US
WHERE CAN WE GO?

Why,
to where we are.

I hold this ivory statuette for you to look at.
It is a carving of you showing something to me.

A
HERO
CHOKING
DRAGONS
ON
A
CLIFF.

Eagle squadrons swirling into stars.

A chariot of hungers all alive with shining eyes.

Starlings squeaking on the rooftops.
A billion points of light.
Black holes catching photons.

Unknown thoughts
(true
muscular
sensations)
going to a masquerade
in strange costumes.
While everything pours outward—steadily and faster!

TILL
WE
GUESS
THAT

Paradise
IS
SMOKE
ABOVE THE FIRE

AND
I
grin

relieved
at
last!

I LOVE YOUR EYES!

DO YOU LOVE MINE?

A
HERO
CHOKING
DRAGONS
ON
A
CLIFF

A
HERO
CHOKING
DRAGONS
ON
A
CLIFF

Blue
macaws . . .

AND SO WE STRETCH OUT . . .
All explosions at the Battle
of Okinawa
or
the
Universe's
core
are
nothing
compared to this shape

I feel
of what I want
but cannot name.

I
prove, by the way things
break me up,
that there is no measure.
I am permanent in change
and all uncarved.

WE FLOAT ALONG.
We are the laughing crest upon the whitecap.

The walls of the cathedral
flood their images. They say

we're going ninety million miles per hour.

The osprey's picture dives across the pond between the cattails.

PUSSYWILLOWS OPEN HERE IN OCTOBER'S IDES!

.

Water strider shadows break up.
Huge claws jar the water's surface
making lines of light on bottom
in the brilliant sun.
The monster's deep-set eyes look at the sky.
Branches of creosote hang from the mouth as he drinks.
The coppery horsehair snake writhes by . . .
Mosquito larvae dive. The painted men
almost giggle
in the rushes.
The sound of water being swallowed in a giant throat.
One man with ochred face and scarlet
eyeholes raises up his
leaf-shaped sword of flint
and kisses it.
He sees
the color that he is
reflected there.
The man with green stripes
trembles sexually
and thinks of blood.
He holds the magic club encrusted with the teeth
and carved with faces.
The tufts of feathers on it drink
flesh juice.
Ochre Head stands
and raises up the flint.

Green Stripes rushes forward with a gleeful scream!
Three snouted creatures in the field beyond the oak trees
raise their heads and peer.

Vultures cock their eyes.

The horsehair snake wriggles in the warm pond water.

The theater we know
is the edges
of our organs,
and
our
selves
are actors.

—Falling through the walls.

HEADS
POKING
DOWN
FROM CEILINGS
—giggling.

THE
POLLYWOG
POND
is
at
the cliff base.
Petrified bones of dinosaurs
hang out above
the tadpoles.
WE
TURN
INTO
TITANS

that
swoop

back
to

our
roots.

We
wear

red
capes

and
sail

through
space.

I
leave
splashes
of
my
radiance

116

adrift
in
everywhere.

Monsters
flee
my
swordpoint.

The white buildings

swoop
upward.

These are my shining scales.

MY
BODY

turns
the many

colors
that

I
know

it
is

and
I

enjoy it!

This
is

where
I

guess
what

shapes

I

grow
to.

Here
I
am
in
a

pocket
grotto
with
all
pressure
turned
inward
to
me.

It
is

not
pain.

HERE
IS

the bison hunt.

Here
are

war
whoops.

Now
is

the
city

on
the

cliff
top.

Here
are
control
switches
miniaturized.

Now
I

choose
to

grow
an

arm
or
leg

120

or to
be
a
Lucifer
or
friendly ghost
of
self

or
a
love
god.

Touch here or *press* there.

BUT LOVE BURSTS!

TO BE A MAN
IS TO BE A MAMMAL-MAN
WITH STYLE
that
does not matter
since all lives are forgotten
when we dissolve in black sugar.
The stately form we had in mind
becomes a turbulence. We learn
that our thoughts
are tiny mountains
and the roots of trees
that we sleep within
stretch through
stellar space.

AND LOVE BURSTS AND THE CREATURE
HULKING OVER US SCREECHES, WHISTLING AIR,
AND PUKES UP WATER, STOPS,
STARES AT US IN WONDER ALMOST HYPNOTIZED
with his own love.
Huge dumb furry face—and giant claws
making magic gestures in the air!
I know he knows that he is dying!
I
WARD THE MAGIC OFF
WITH A THOUGHT!
He bares his chest
and I leap up with the flint sword!
My face is ochre.
His
shit
pours
into
the
pond.
His red blood dissolves the osprey's picture
in the waves.

AND I BREAK OUT AND CRY IN LONG
FORGOTTEN SONGS!

HE STANDS WITH THE FLINT STUCK IN HIM.

HE IS I—AND I AM HIM.
WE ARE THE RIVER POURING TO THE ROOTS
THAT FEED THE BLOSSOM!

WE ARE THE RIVER!

WE ARE THE RIVER!

OUR FACES ARE THE WAVES!

Printed January 1974 in Santa Barbara for the Black Sparrow Press by Noel Young. Design by Barbara Martin. This edition is published in paper wrappers; there are 200 hardcover copies numbered & signed by the poet; & 26 lettered copies handbound in boards by Earle Gray signed & with an original drawing by the poet.

Michael McClure is also well known as a playwright, as *The Beard* is now recognized as one of the most important plays of the 1960's. More recently, McClure has also published a bizarre collection of plays called *Gargoyle Cartoons,* and two novels, *The Mad Cub* and *The Adept.* He is currently working on a long essay about biological systems, and is touring the world to enlarge his vision of man in his various attempts to push away from his substrate.

Michael McClure's first published poems were two villanelles for Roethke published in *Poetry* in 1956. Since then he has been constantly enlarging his craft, expanding out into and creating new forms as he simultaneously follows closely the evolution of his personal vision. *Rare Angel* is a complex interwoven journey through that personal universe.